"Suicide to Success"

How a locked Exit gave me a Way Out!

By Rob Goddard

"Suicide to Success"

By Rob Goddard

(First Edition)

Forward

This book is intended to help anyone that finds life's journey all too much and wants to give up.

It's especially aimed at Entrepreneurs who sometimes find running their own business overwhelming, all demanding and perhaps very lonely at times.

You may have even experienced business failure and a dismantling of your personal life. Often the two are inextricably intertwined.

If you are like me, you will have practised or even perfected the art of only showing to the outside world what you want them to see. Perhaps you have built a "superhero suit" that others perceive you by, but they don't get to see the "real" you.

Somehow, and rather mistakenly, many of us believe that if we make ourselves open to others, we become weaker and more vulnerable as a person.

In writing this book, I have made myself vulnerable to you, sharing my personal journey the highs and the lows. Only when we open up to others do we really gain strength to cope with what life throws at us and get to grips with its many twists and turns.

This is not a book on how to get rich quick. Instead, it centres around how to dig deep, persevere, build your self-esteem and inner confidence.

It will also hopefully show how people can come into your life at just the right moment. Events happening at just the right time, serendipity at work in my life, as indeed it may well happen in your own life.

Contrary to what they taught when I was at school, do feel free to write your own notes and thoughts in this book. Make the book come alive with your own experiences and thoughts and most importantly what you plan to do to take back control of your life.

Contents

Dedication

Without my four wonderful children, Tom, Josh, Haydn and Phoenix, life would lack the meaning that it does.

I'm not the "perfect" Dad, but I love each of them so very much. My four wonderful children may never know how much or how deeply.

A very special mention to my wife, Liz, who has been a constant source of support and encouragement, which has also inspired me to write this book.

They are the reason I am still here to write this book.

With much love.

Did you know?

That suicide stands as the single biggest killer of men under the age of 45, with 4,623 men recorded as taking their own lives in 2014. That's one every two hours!

41% of men who contemplated suicide didn't feel they could talk about their feelings.

Sources:

Jane Powell (CEO) of CALM
YouGov Poll
Office for National Statistics

Chapter 1 – thwarted by Architects

I travelled up to the 163rd floor of Dubai's Burj Khalifa, with the intent of throwing myself off the top of it, in 2010.

Half a mile up in the air, I calculated that I would probably die long before I hit the ground and have the added benefit of no repatriation costs since there wouldn't be much of me left to collect!

This all sounds rather macabre, but when you're in a severely depressed state of mind logic and rational thinking take a back seat. It's more about finishing the pain, anguish, anxiety and the utter turmoil of life.

There seems to be no other option but to end your own life. At least that is one thing you can take control of when the rest of world seems to control you and how you feel.

What I didn't appreciate was that, unfortunately, in the Burj Khalifa it is all floor to ceiling glass windows and so there is no way of jumping over the top of a barrier to plunge to one's death. I'm guessing that astute Architects of such wonderful buildings and structures take into account that one day some deranged or mad person may just decide to jump from the top.

I wasn't put off by this architectural safety design, so I started looking for another way, a fire exit leading to the outside maybe?

Yes, I was in luck! There was indeed a fire exit door, so I quickly made for it but found, to my utter dismay, that it was locked. Who on earth locks a fire exit, for goodness sake! The people that maintain the building clearly do and, much to my eternal gratitude, they certainly did on that day.

So how did I get to the point of wanting to end it all after 45 years on this planet and how did I turn things around to achieve personal and business success?

Well, you will need to read on!

Chapter 2 – Life in a commune

I left college at 18 and went into what was a very respectable career in banking. I was good with numbers and also wanted my Mum to be proud of me.

In those days, being a Bank Manager was something to which to aspire. Not these days of course but, back in the early 80s, a Bank Manager was one of the three pillars of a business community, along with Lawyers and Accountants.

So began a 16-year career in Banking in which I progressed through the ranks to reach the heady heights of Senior Manager in the mid-90s. Towards those later years, however, I became more restless and disillusioned with the Banking sector. It seemed far too restrictive and rule driven for me. Free expression, initiative, and spontaneity weren't high up the list of corporate priorities for an established high street Bank, that was far more driven by maintaining the status quo and ensuring conformity.

So in 1998 I left, with my wife Sharon and our twin boys (Tom and Josh), to live in a suburb of Los Angeles called Chino, to work in a Christian Food Ministry feeding 700/800 low-income or homeless people, largely Hispanics. Both Sharon and I had been active members of a UK church and in fact, that's how we met originally.

So undertaking this type of work was part of our religious calling and beliefs and Sharon's cousins led a small but dynamic church in this town. We had been to this LA church previously on a month's holiday and fell in love with the sense of purpose and real service to the community it provided. It was also "on the edge" Christianity that had immense appeal, especially for me.

It couldn't have been further from the Banking industry.

Chino is not on the tourist trail. It's primarily known for two things, cows and a state penitentiary. This was no adventure to the glitzy world of Los Angeles - "La La land" as it's affectionately referred to.

It was going to be hard work living in neighbourhoods with drive-by shootings and wide-spread poverty.

Our sons were only 2-years old at the time, and so they knew nothing of the change of life and upheaval that we had made, but they loved being part of a commune with 90+ church people, of which, 30 or so were other children. One big nursery school for them! Unlimited children to play with and numerous "Mothers" to look after them. They became "Community Kids", looked after and loved by many others in the group.

It was also a real "boot camp" experience for me leaving a well-paid job and respected career to be a ministry worker for a small church overseas. Feeding, supporting and being friends with many forgotten and unwanted local people was a very humbling experience.

We went into many local communities with a truck loaded with tonnes of produce, bagging it up and handing out food on the streets.

We had a rule, that we gave as much food as they could carry. Life in its raw state and making a difference to others.

Christmas especially was an extravaganza. An amazing 20,000+ donated toys sorted into gender and age groups, we even ended up renting an old Bank of America building for a $1 a month to store and distribute all these gifts. There was something ironic in going back into a bank, this time to give, not to take.

Our outreach work into the community was so respected that sometimes local gang members kept guard, making sure there were no disturbances on the streets and that everyone waited in line quietly.

We even went to a place called "skid row" in central Los Angeles to give out clothing, food and to sing a variety of choruses to the homeless and the forgotten in society.

There was talk of a former "Sex Pistol" Glen Matlock accompanying us on guitar one evening at "skid row." I was a Pistols fan, but he didn't look much like Glen at all.

My wife and I were given $10 a week plus free food and accommodation. Basic living, but no different to the people we were serving in the communities. You can live on very little. What matters is the support and love of the people around you.

When we weren't distributing food I was working with other guys undertaking landscape and gardening maintenance work for the middle classes in and around Los Angeles.

What did I know about gardening? Absolutely nothing, but I did lose several stones in weight working in temperatures of 35 degrees or more!   The enjoyment of gardening stays with me to this day.

After this 8-month experience we returned home, having discovered some practices within the Church that we did not agree with.

So without a job to go to, or even a home, we headed back to the UK. We had sold up everything to work overseas and now returned unexpectedly back to Britain, although nothing in life is ever wasted.

Back in the UK we both still had a longing to make a difference somehow in life. What I didn't know at the time was this lifestyle experience was preparing me for other experiences in life and it also softened my heart up to people. Looking back, I think that commercial life had caused me to become rather hard-hearted and selfish in life.

My learning: *If life has become tedious and lacking in challenges, change it!*

How does that relate to you?

What action(s) will you take?

Chapter 3 – starting over again

Within weeks of returning from Los Angeles, miraculously we found a home and I found a job. We had the love and support of our home church in the UK which was instrumental in us integrating back into "normal" life.

However, we didn't want "normal," we wanted to use our experience as a springboard for life back in the UK.

I got a job on £11k a year plus bonuses, which was significantly higher than $10 a week back in Chino! It was a telesales job but I really hated the thought of cold calling. I've always avoided such work, but it was that or nothing, so I threw myself into it, especially as we had rent, other bills to pay and two young children to feed. I spent 4 years in the company and in that time become Head of Operations.

What I discovered, from my time there, was that I really liked being part of a small privately-owned company. I knew life in the corporate world wasn't for me anymore. Being involved in a more flexible and fast-growing environment was much more exciting and satisfying.

During my time with the company, I was involved in helping to raise $20m from Private Equity for the UK business to set up in the States. I was firmly back in the world of business, but this time working for a rapidly growing Small to Medium-sized Enterprise (SME).

I liked the nature of an SME; you could make a notable difference without too much red tape and bureaucracy. It was also easier to demonstrate your personal contribution to overall growth of the company.

In banking, you are a very small cog in a huge wheel. You get lost in the 'machinery teeth' of a bank.

Encouraged by this personal renaissance in business, in 2002 I decided to devise a fifteen-year plan to retire at 55, move to Greece and teach English to Greek children. Why Greece, you might ask? Well, I was looking for somewhere warm, with a slower pace of life. It also need to be close enough to fly back to the UK to visit the family.

Why Teach? I saw it as a "passport to working in another country. I qualified as a teacher under the TEFL scheme and taught a part-time evening class for two years at a local college to practice my new found abilities. I loved it!

It wasn't so much the teaching of a language, it was more the interaction with other people and sharing things, about British life and culture, which was most rewarding. Also, it was learning about other cultures in the classroom, Polish, Czech, Albanian, Romanian, Chinese and Japanese. I encouraged students to share information about their own country and customs too.

It was in that same year that I was approached by another privately-owned company, a well-established Mergers and Acquisition firm, that had plans for significant growth. They asked me to join as General Manager to help deliver that growth, which I did; a 10-fold increase in sales within 7 years, as it turned out.

It was a fantastic experience which brought out qualities and skills that I didn't know I had, such as "entrepreneurialism."

In other words, I found I could make things happen and make money, not only for myself but for other people, shareholders, staff and clients. At last, I had found a career that suited me to the ground.

I was totally unaware of the range of skills I had developed when I was in Banking. Yes, I was good at selling, but this was different. Working in a small but growing business was more about having a vision, organising resources and making it happen. It was also about having a "nose" for good business and generating attractive profits from sometimes limited resources.

As business success grew, so did my personal income. I ended up in the top 1% of earners in the country. The trouble was, my over-confidence and materialistic side took over.

The time I worked in the Los Angeles commune feeding the poor and all the learnings from that were subsequently smothered by materialism, self-interest and advancement. I believed my own "hype" and I was soon going to learn that things can be taken away in an instant, and it did dramatically in 2008.

My learning: *You can do anything in life, just not everything.*

How does that relate to you?

What action(s) will you take?

Chapter 4 – the collapse of my world

During the 2nd half of 2008, I lost my job, my home and my marriage. All down to me; no-one else's fault but mine. It was an earth shattering moment in my life that rocked the very foundation of my world.

The life I had taken decades to build and nurture was blown away in a matter of a few months and worse still, by my own stupid actions. This is not the book to go into detail of what occurred, but suffice to say, I lost sight of what was important in my life at that time.

Our lives can be very fragile, often we think they are robust and built on rock. It's often not, more like it's built on shifting sands sometimes.

In less than 10 years I had changed from feeding the poor as a missionary to an ego-centric businessman. I'm not entirely sure how that transition happened, but happen it did.

The pursuit of career and money became intoxicating and exciting for me. It was like a drug. I was going into shops not needing to know the price of something. I bought a series of brand new Harley Davidson's and luxury cars. On one cruise I bought a dozen original paintings on board the ship at an auction. The bill, slipped under the cabin door the night before disembarkation, was eye-watering, even for me! Money had very little value because I had so much of it.

The trouble is also that we can often surround ourselves with "things" to make us happy and content. Symbols that life is good to us and that we are successful. This is, in fact, an illusion.

Happiness, contentment and true success come from somewhere else. Somewhere deep down from within us. An inner knowledge that we are at peace with who we are and can enjoy being in the "moment." The Eastern religions understand something about this.

"If you love someone, the greatest gift you can give them is your presence. If you love someone but rarely make yourself available to him or her, that is not true love. The most precious gift we can offer anyone is our attention. When mindfulness embraces those we love, they will bloom like flowers."
-    Thich Nhat Hanh

You can't buy happiness and contentment, only experience it.

My life in 2008 was far from this utopian existence, I became jobless with huge debts circling like vultures and I had separated from my wife leaving her behind living at home with my two sons. Words are difficult to express the pain of separation, especially from your own children. It's the pain I inflicted on them that was the most difficult to bear because they were not at fault, but nevertheless had become victims in a situation that I created.

To this day, I still carry that guilt with me. We often think our Dad is infallible, my sons sadly discovered that I was not.

I went into a deep spiral emotionally and mentally, was prescribed a collection of drugs and was also asked to fill in a form by my Doctor concerning my mental state. One of the questions was, *"have you had, or do you have, thoughts of suicide or harming yourself."* I answered truthfully, "yes." I knew at that point I was in a very bad way.

Admitting I was prepared to end my life and disappear from the world made it real to me that I was suffering from severe depression.

I hadn't admitted it to myself until that point. I had always viewed people with depression as "weak minded." Now I was experiencing it for myself and I knew I wasn't weak minded.

The depression for me was like a dark ominous cloud that invaded my world whenever it chose, enveloping my space and my thoughts. The array of medicines helped, eventually, to stabilise my condition but, in three years of taking them, they never helped get rid of my depression. I recall reading the notes they always insert in the boxes of tablets and being rather bemused by the statement that one of the side effects of taking these anti-depressants was that it might cause depression!

Being in the state of mind that life is not worth living and the world doesn't really care is a very scary place. Loneliness and isolation became part of my condition, as did extreme anxiety and panic about the future. It becomes a vicious cycle and wasn't helped by me renting single rooms on a short term basis.

I wasn't eating properly, instead, I was consuming alcohol to "self-medicate" when my body started to get used to the effects of the prescribed drugs. It was a spiral I felt I couldn't break and so turned to the internet to look up ways of killing myself, ideally without any pain. I recall being astounded at a number of articles out there on suicide.

I came to the conclusion there was no guaranteed way of dying without pain.

One post struck me at the time, it said, *"Suicide is a long-term solution to a short-term problem."* I think that sunk into my subconscious somehow.

I came to move in with a close friend, Lisa, with whom I had a daughter, Haydn, and subsequently had a second daughter, Phoenix. It was extremely hard for Lisa, she did her best to support and encourage me but I was damaged goods, mentally and emotionally.

I got into the habit of watching a lot of Jeremy Kyle in the mornings, so I could forget how bad my life really was. It was somewhat entertaining and also my life didn't seem so dire compared to most of the people that go on that show.

"Come Dine with me" was also a favourite of mine then, a bit of escapism for an hour from the depressing world I inhabited. I loved the narrator's humour and I like cooking, so a good combination.

I got myself into some basic routines that weren't too onerous and stopped me, even for a short while, dwelling on my depression.

However, I wasn't bouncing back to my normal self; it was just existence, not living. As the months ticked by, I was not improving and so Lisa encouraged me to see a Psychotherapist. The combined Cognitive Behavioural Therapy and Hypnotherapy did help to a degree, as did the opportunity to talk each week with a complete stranger about my overwhelming problems.

One technique I was taught was to visualise myself in a plastic sphere protected from what was outside, contained in my own bubble, but I could see and hear what was going on outside but somehow it didn't affect me. This made me feel empowered. That my own space around me couldn't be affected by life. It was my space, unaffected by others. It was as if I had some degree of control back in my life, something to build on.

My learning: My life was centred on the wrong priorities. I needed to build on rock, not sand.

How does that relate to you?

What action(s) will you take?

Chapter 5 – rebuilding

It was also at this time I set up my own business, offering business consultancy and advice. After all, no-one was going to employ me in this state! I never in my life wanted to work for myself but I had no choice, the employment market was pretty much dead and I had some chunky bills to pay. My previous employer also said they would contract my services for a while.

I started my new business from my bedroom with a broadband connection, a basic website and some business cards. I then networked like hell. No-one knew I was out there, what I offered and how I might be able to help them.

I felt a fraud, though. I had no business really, I was just starting out on my own and I was contemplating suicide on a near daily basis. I can even remember breaking down into tears as I was driving to one networking event in Newbury. Uncontrollable tears about what life had become for me and how there was no hope left.

It was at this event that I met a guy called Alex Petty. Alex subsequently became a more important figure in my life than just another person at a business networking event, but I didn't know that at the time.

Alex's opening question to me was *"what can I do to help you grow your business?"* No-one has ever asked me that. It was an insightful question and it was focused on me, rather than him. A good tactic at networking events.

He made me think for a moment and I said that I had just started out on my own and looking for new business leads. Alex then asked how many do you need? Another great question! I said I didn't know how many I needed, I didn't even have a strategy, a plan, or financial forecast and budgets.

Alex was part of a national business coaching group and I found that their 90-day planning events he introduced me to were fantastic and just what I needed at the time.

It gave me focus, tactics and strategy for the next three months ahead. As was Alex's wise counsel on things from the sidelines. I learnt that to set up in business, you need a vision, a plan and someone you trust to act as a sounding board. With that platform, you can do anything and the best part is it doesn't have to cost you much at all, just time and effort.

I can recall one meeting with Alex, in his office, where we mapped out what I really wanted in life. We put a lot of things on the wipe board, I remember a few things I'd written down, like a six-figure income and a successful business that I could sell one day and then retire early. I also stated that I wanted real happiness and contentment in my life.

The reality though was that I had 3 weeks' cash left before I ran out of money and so needed new business income fast. Also, the large investment bank, Lehman Brothers had just collapsed, the banking crisis erupted and the world entered into what became a long and deep recession. Coupled with coping with my own personal turmoil, it was not an ideal time to set up a business but I did it. I had no real choice since state benefits wouldn't cover a fraction of my bills.

Given I didn't have much in the way of a marketing budget, I hit the free networking events, used LinkedIn, set up a basic database from which I could undertake rudimentary mailshots and I contacted anyone that I had met in the past letting them know what I was up to and what I could offer. I also had someone set up a basic website, I couldn't afford much more.

My previous employer also offered retained consultancy work to me which was a godsend. It gave me a flow of cash that enabled me to rent a small office in Newbury from a good friend, Mia, who ran a successful recruitment business in Newbury. It felt like a "proper" business having an office to work from, rather than a bedroom.

The office also had the benefit of me mixing and socialising daily with other people. It got me out of the house, the heavy drinking and daytime TV. Mia was also very easy to chat with about business, life and the universe.

I hired my first employee, Kristina. Kristina was another friend and former language student, she came in one day a week to populate the database with new records and information. Kristina was my formative marketing department and also emotional support. It was us against the rest of the world!

So three people in my life were keeping me anchored, Alex, Mia and Kristina. They cared about me and I drew great strength from that - more than they will ever know.

Some happiness and laughter was starting to creep back into my life. I wasn't quite out of the woods yet. I was still on medication and still drinking too much, but there was some hope, some light at the end of the tunnel starting to gleam.

My learning: Finding a few true friends is worth far more than having hundreds of acquaintenances.

How does that relate to you?

What action(s) will you take?

Chapter 6 – setbacks

In the first year running my own business, it made a £110k turnover in its first year, which made me feel delighted. I had plans then to grow it into a multi-million pound empire within three years, perhaps naively. Then I received news that my largest client was going to cancel their retained work because of the recession - I was gobsmacked!

All my plans for future growth had assumed that this client, which represented 70%+ of my business revenues, would always loyally be there with me on my journey. I learnt a very harsh lesson in business life.

My world was again rocked in little over a year. I felt that the short term success that had been achieved had been cruelly stolen from me and, in doing so, my fledgeling hope in life had been taken with it too. So I spiralled downward once again.

Depression, helplessness and no self-worth came flooding back to haunt me.

I therefore decided I wasn't going to take my prescription tablets regularly, I was going to save them up and take them in one go and bring an end to this painful life. For once I was going to be in control of my fortunes, not external events or other people. Instead of medication, I took alcohol to dull the pain and depression. I ended up keeping those pills for many years, there were over 700 of them in the end.

I came across an advert for a Financial Planning job in Dubai. It was commission only but I had been an Independent Financial Adviser in the past and what could be easier than selling financial products to some of the richest people in the world? I had nothing to lose and I could still run my own (much smaller) UK business remotely, from Dubai.

I applied for the job, got it and within 6 weeks had rocked up in the Middle East eager to start work. I had been promised a database and leads from the company I was working for. I got neither. What I did get was a twenty-something Boss who had been out there for 4 years, had the trappings of success and thought he knew everything about selling.

I'm sure he was as disappointed with me because he was given someone twice his age that didn't agree with many of his sales and business techniques. I suspected it wasn't going to go well in Dubai.

I started to think that I may have jumped from the frying pan into the fire, quite literally with temperatures above 45 degrees centigrade in summer.

Still, I had made the decision and so I was determined to make the most of it. The problem with a commission only job in a place like Dubai is that your cash runs out pretty quickly if you don't get some early success. It's a 5-star lifestyle but that takes a lot of money to fund it. That's fine if you are employed and receiving £1m+ in salary and paying no tax.

But, if you are self-employed, and not knowing where the next commission cheque is coming from, that can be a disaster. Also, people that can't pay their bills get put into jail, as it is a criminal offence in Dubai to owe money.

That all makes for a highly pressured environment to work in and I still had a small legacy business to service back in the UK, so working round the clock in different time zones wasn't easy. It was also hard being 3,000 miles away from my support network, Kristina, Alex and Mia.

With them being so far away I was once again on my own in what was a very harsh, uncompromising and unforgiving environment.

I can remember waking up most mornings feeling in a panic, having waves of anxiety, then throwing up in the sink. It became a ritual affair before putting on my suit and going to the office in my little hired Toyota car. I put a brave face on every day, not wanting others, especially my boss, to be aware of the anguish and turmoil I was in.

This time, it felt worse. Here I was suffering from depression, away from the people closest to me in a foreign country and in a new job, without any certainty of income.

My learning: Don't get complacent. Think about contigency should things not work out the way you plan.

How does that relate to you?

What action(s) will you take?

Chapter 7 – Dubai, brave new world

Without the promised database of prospects, the flow of leads or a brand, I needed to generate new clients and fast, as my tiny apartment alone was costing me £3,000 per month.

I used LinkedIn, connected with hundreds of people in Dubai and then started sending out informative articles related to financial planning. I also started hanging out in places my target audience would frequent, the Dubai Marina, the Irish Bar, and a whole manner of networking groups. I even travelled up and down the country's only arterial motorway, the Sheikh Zayed Road. It is 400 miles long with 6 lanes on each carriageway.

Dubai has a plethora of motor dealerships alongside this monstrous motorway, Ferrari, Maserati, Rolls-Royce, Porsche, and Harley Davidson to name but a few.

These were all places my target market would spend their time and money.

I cold called all the dealerships in Dubai, it took me two months, and I offered a free financial planning review as a bolt-on service to automotive customers of those dealerships. Many said "no" but a few said "yes" and one even gave me 1,200 email addresses of customers they had in the UAE, which I could use for my own marketing.

Bear in mind that there was no Financial Services Act nor Data Protection legislation, certainly not in Dubai at that time. It was like the "Wild West" out there, everyone for themselves, a chance to make big money for those that worked hard and were determined to succeed. I also think my ability to focus and single-mindedness were helpful attributes.

I can remember one sales call I made was to a Partner in a large law firm, he finished the meeting by writing out a personal cheque for £300,000 to invest in a product I was offering and then introduced me to his Managing Partner who ended up writing another cheque for the same amount.

I walked out from their plush offices with £600,000 and instantly calculated my commission on those two transactions. I was exhilarated and thrilled, I was back on track, I had conquered Dubai, or so I thought.

The problem is that those successes aren't every week, but your bills and financial commitments do come all too regularly. The immense stress of having to sign people up was overwhelming.

I worked round the clock, didn't eat anything apart from chicken and salami, washed down with a lot, and I mean a lot, of vodka and tonic.

Dubai is not a "dry" country, you just need to know where to get it. The Duty-Free shop in the airport is a good start. It does seem ironic that one of the first things you can buy when you land in Dubai is alcohol.

Stress, anxiety and being alone all took its toll on me. I started frequenting those suicide websites again and contemplated ending it all in Dubai. Go out with a bang by jumping off the tallest building in the world, the Burj Khalifa. No repatriation costs, as there wouldn't have been anything left of me to send back to Britain. I would save my family $25,000 in costs.

I also kept a "death diary," writing down all my thoughts as they came to me, something to leave behind after I had gone to hopefully give understanding to my family and close friends why I had decided to kill myself.

It sounds a weird thing to do, but it mattered to me that there was some sort of explanation to my actions.

It also turned out to be a useful way of helping to get thoughts racing in my mind onto paper. A kind of therapy I suppose.

Also, it showed me over a number of months, what things were important to me and that the impact of my suicide on my four children would be dreadful. They would probably never forgive me. The key reason I kept going and didn't give into suicide was my children. Looking back and when I boil it all down, it was what effect would it have on them, knowing their Dad had done such an awful thing and left them behind.

So I was really torn and in immense anguish between digging in or just giving up and letting gravity do its work.

I did go to the Burj Khalifa with the intent of ending my life. It's 830m. high and jumping off it would certainly be final. Were it not for a locked fire exit door, I may not be writing this book.

If it had been open, as it should have been, who knows whether I would have gone ahead and committed suicide. It's one of those things in life one can never know.

What I do know is that I wasn't given the choice to end my life that day.

After my thwarted attempt at the Burj, I returned back to my apartment and was at a loss as to what I should do.

My learning: Sometimes life's circumstances are telling you don't give up, just find another solution.

How does that relate to you?

What action(s) will you take?

Chapter 8 – phone a friend

I had kept in touch with my friend Alex whilst I was in Dubai and so skyped him asking if he wanted to come over for a few days, at my expense. Never one to let an offer like that go begging, Alex was on a flight to the Gulf in the blink of an eye.

I never mentioned to him my aborted suicide attempt, but when he arrived he guessed that I was not in a good way. Those few days together were a real lifeline for me.

I remember him looking in my fridge saying, *"There's nothing green in your fridge! Just meat and alcohol!"* Who needs Jiminy Cricket, when you have Alex around? Apart from the dietary advice that he freely gave to me, we also pontificated about life, the universe and everything, sat on sun lounges at the pool on top of my apartment.

One key question he posed was, *"what is it you want, really want to do in business life?"* My reply was that I wanted to return back to selling businesses for other people.

So then began a creative planning session, by the pool, as to how that might happen. Once more a little hope returned that things might take a turn for the better. You only need to see a speck of light at the end of the tunnel to make your way towards it.

Shortly after Alex flew back an old friend of mine, Chris Barker, got in contact with me. He was on holiday in Dubai and suggested we get together for a beer, or three. We hadn't seen each other for 25 years when I was "best man" at his wedding. We lost touch over time, but here he was in the Dubai desert, like me. Meeting him again was excellent. It was as if nothing had changed and we immediately picked up where we had left off. We did some fun things like Go-Kart racing and enjoying the night life of Dubai. I hadn't done anything fun since I landed in the country; it was all work and certainly no play. Chris changed that.

The third person who helped me survive in the Gulf, albeit unwittingly, was Andrew Prince. Andrew is a highly respected IFA who had spent several years working in Dubai. He was looking to work for the company I was working for and I remember we had a chat about my experiences of the company in question and I recall saying don't join us, stay where you are. He promptly ignored my advice and joined us the following week – and I'm so pleased that he did.

Andrew and I had numerous coffee time chats, lunch in the local Lebanese cafe and a beer in the evening. We are of a similar age so it was refreshing to talk with someone on the same level. He also has a dry, sometimes acerbic wit, which I like. He was the voice of reason in a mad environment. We became good friends and have remained so since.

Without thinking, I had built my small support network in the UAE, just like I had done in the UK. You only need one or two good friends to help you cope with life. It's not the multitude that will help, it's a few special people that happen to come into your life at the right time. The multitude tend to ignore you when you need them.

It became clear that life in Dubai was not for me. So over Ramadan period I wrote to twenty Accountancy firms and said I was an experienced Corporate Finance person currently in the Middle East, looking to return back to the UK, do you have a role for me?

Surprisingly, five firms responded positively and I flew back to the UK for interviews. The one I eventually decided to go with wasn't an employed position, it was to set up a new business with me as a shareholder and Managing Director. We all put money in but I was the only one working in the business - Evolution Complete Business Sales Ltd was born.

Top of the Burj Khalifa

Looking down from the Burj Khalifa

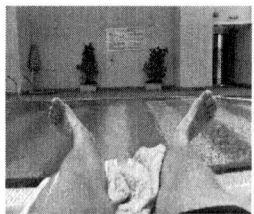

The moment my new business was devised

Chapter 9 – confidence

In February 2011 my new business, Evolution CBS Ltd, was born. I had thirteen other investors on board and a vision for the future. Setting up in business is never easy and especially setting one up during a recession.

However, the support and encouragement from my investors was extremely helpful and valuable. For once, I didn't feel alone in business. I had other people around me with convergent interests.

My previous experiences of working as a "one-man band" and then working without a salary in a foreign country stood me in good stead. I had unwittingly developed skills, of survival, resourcefulness and creativity, I would never have discovered had I remained in banking. I truly felt that the last few years had been an apprenticeship for something more substantive in my business life.

The issue I had to contend with was feeling a bit of a fraud. A new business, without a track record, just me and my ever-present depression. But I did have a smile and enthusiasm, yet I knew that wasn't going to be enough. I needed something else - I needed self-confidence. One thing that often evaporates when you suffer from depression is your own self-worth. True, you can pretend to be confident, project confidence, but many see through it.

Whilst searching the internet, I found a "Confidence Coach", Tracey Miller, to help me in this area. I would go into panic mode before a sales pitch or a presentation for an event. Tracey was fabulous, she let me talk and talk, just asking me pertinent questions from time to time. She helped me to face my deep fears in life over a period of a few months. Tracey also tapped into my long term life goal of being on a Greek island, teaching English when I hit 55 years of age.

She helped me see that it wasn't just dealing with the issues of today; it was about setting my sights on the future and having wonderful and exciting goals and ambitions to achieve in life.

Tracey and her partner George Swift are two of the most inspiring people I have met. I have been part of their BBB Success Group and more latterly their Mastermind Group in Berkshire. Forums where like-minded business owners share their business problems and their successes in a supportive and positive environment. It can be lonely at the top, so it's really important to link up with other peers.

One key aspect I've discovered is that it's okay to be yourself. People like authenticity and naturalness, they respond positively to it. Being human is a natural state to be in. For too many years I had tried to pretend to be someone I wasn't.

Being myself, warts 'n' all, is a good state of mind. I found that I enjoyed "being in the moment". In other words recognising and enjoying the things around me rather than striving and dashing from one thing to another, without truly experiencing them.

My learning: Past failures can help equip you for the future.

How does that relate to you?

What action(s) will you take?

Chapter 10 – onwards and upwards

So there I was, in early 2011, with a new business called Evolution CBS, but it was different this time. I had some working capital from investors so I could pay myself a salary from day one. This meant that I had time to do the right things in the right order. Planning and preparation could be done properly.

Do you know that more than one in three business start-ups never see their 3rd anniversary? A common failing is the lack of proper planning and market research. Too many business owners just jump in and start burning cash on initiatives and things that turn out to be mistakes. Unless you have deep pockets and love this fly by the seat of your pants approach, a more considered and planned approach is far preferable.

Here's a checklist of questions to address in a business plan;

1. What exactly are you offering to the market?
2. What problem does it solves?
3. Why would someone would buy it?
4. Who else offers something similar?
5. Why should someone choose to buy from you, rather than elsewhere?
6. Create a realistic and prudent 3-year growth plan of anticipated sales and related costs.
7. Make sure too that you have sufficient working capital. Whatever you believe you need, add another 50%.
8. What is your "plan B" if it goes wrong?

My goal was to create a £million business within 5 years. I also wanted to return back to my long-term goal of retiring at the age of 55 and teach English from a Greek island.

There is something healthy about having a longer term plan for your own life, not just make money from growing a business. Money is purely a short term motivator; it does not satisfy in the long term. I've experienced this in my own life. I've been rich and I've been poor at different points in my life, several times. Possessions count for very little in reality; it's a significance and purpose in life that matter far more. It's a reason to get up on a Monday morning with an excitement for the week; a sense that what you are doing matters to someone or something.

So, I had a vision, a plan and financial backing, now I had to make it happen. I believed that I could make it happen since I had been through the mill in setting up two micro businesses previously, one in 2008 and the other in 2010 in Dubai. I had learnt skills and tactics that would help me in growing my new business, Evolution CBS, along with 7 years' experience of selling businesses for another brokerage. I had confidence that, with my expertise built up in the industry, it would be successful.

Self-confidence is a key attribute for many successful business owners. You need to believe that you are right and that success will follow. The other quality that should follow is the ability to listen to the wise counsel of others. In my experience, this is often harder for business owners to embrace, particularly if they have encountered some success.

Why should they listen to the advice of others if what they are doing is already working well?

This thinking can be a pitfall since the success may not have been down to the owner, they could have just got lucky, right place, right time. Also, who is to say that more success could have been achieved in the past if other people's input and thoughts had been asked for and included?

It's something I still tussle with. My starting point in my head is that I know what needs to be done to make something work and it's down to others to show or prove to me that there is a better way. It's not an ideal mindset I would admit, but I am a work in progress on that front.

Chapter 11 – how to create success

Hopefully, you have not just turned to this chapter without reading the preceding chapters. If you have, go back to the beginning as it will mean more and provide context. There are no get rich quick plans that work. It's grit, determination, previous failures, serendipity and a little bit of luck that creates a successful business.

The blueprint for the growth of Evolution CBS came from reading the "Beermat Entrepreneur". I needed to establish four pillars to the business, with me at the centre. Those four pillars would in time become the Senior Team that would run the business day to day, and help release me as the owner to be on the business, not in it, as Michael Gerber would say ("The E-Myth" – is another inspirational book for me.)

I wanted to start with the initial pillar of Marketing. You can be a fantastic sales person but if you don't have a good flow of qualified leads you are sunk. So my first hire was Kay. She came highly recommend to me by our mutual friend, Mia, so no recruitment fee! What appealed to me about Kay was that she was an accomplished marketing person with extensive commercial experience and she had run her own business successfully for 7 years.

She's proven to be a first class hire, highly professional, knowledgeable, flexible and a real grafter. For a while it was just me and Kay working together, she would create visibility for the business, generating leads and I would follow them up and start to secure new retained clients.

After a number of months, it became clear that I needed a 2nd pillar, that of Operations. I couldn't sell and then at the same time undertake delivery of the service. For that, I engaged two people, James and Claire, both of whom had worked for me before, in the same industry, so I had first-hand experience of their strengths and weaknesses. They were both available at the right time, so again no recruitment fees at all.

The 3rd pillar of the business, Finance, was provided by my investors, as they were Accountants. I have learnt so much over the years from them about financial reporting and interpretation of the figures. To know your numbers gives you comfort and you can sleep at night.

I meet too many fellow business owners that do not have a clue how much money their business is making.

They don't budget for the year and they don't review the financial performance monthly. I want to sleep at night knowing there is a sufficient cash buffer in the bank (say 3 months) and that there will be no unwelcome surprises with unexpected bills surfacing.

If an owner says "I'm not an Accountant" my response is always that you don't need to be. You just need to be on top of your own numbers as part of being a competent Director. Remember, you can make a loss a number of times, but you can only run out of cash once!

The 4th pillar is Sales, but not me selling. For that, I turned to my old boss from my banking days, Steve. He was a person I looked to for sales coaching and inspiration. He's the commensurate deal closer and when he became available, I approached him. No recruitment agency involved again.

Engaging someone to take on the new Business Development side from me was critical. A business reliant on the owner's skills and involvement is worth far less than one that isn't. One of our roles as an owner is to bring into the business people that are better than we are. To effectively make ourselves redundant from our own businesses.

Business acquirers avoid purchasing owner-reliant businesses. Or, if they do, it's at a heavily discounted price. To them, it's like buying a car without an engine.

Also, don't think that, as the outgoing owner, you can stay on for a couple of years under new ownership. It rarely works, after all, when was the last time you had a boss? Someone who can tell you "no" and do as you are told.

Evolution is a four pillar business now, just as in the book I read. We've also employed others along the way, each with specific skills and something valuable to add to the growing team and not one has cost me a recruitment agency fee – I bet you are spotting a trend here!

All of them have either worked for me before or been highly recommended by a trusted source.

The hardest transition I've found in growing a business is letting go of the day to day running. When you have cash invested, plus blood, sweat and tears, it's not easy at all to let others in the team run the business. Many business owners feel that no-one can run their business as well as they do. That may be true in some cases but without delegation and empowerment of key staff the business will surely plateau in performance - it always does.

This is because there are only 7 days in the week even for us business owners.

The secret to growing a successful business is to find the right people, trust them and supply sufficient resources to help them achieve their targets.

As owners, we are there primarily to set direction, monitor results and make the big decisions within the business. It's tempting to interfere but this must be resisted at all costs.

So where is the business today? Well, I recently bought out my original investors. There is a season for everything and the time had come to part company. It's not uncommon to have divergent interests at Board level, very normal in fact. The business was valued at £1.5m, not bad from a cold start, during a recession and in just 5 years or so.

I have become CEO, the business has repaid the original loan to me and I have brought in 3 new investors, each of whom has something fresh to bring to the table for the next phase in Evolution's growth cycle.

The last few pages have been the mechanics behind how I grew my business from scratch and into something sustainable, profitable and scalable.

The other key element is my inner drive and determination to win through. A "whatever it takes" mentality to ensure that success prevails. I've often been accused of being stubborn. Well, I think it's an asset when starting and growing your own business. The complete conviction that what you're doing is right and will succeed over a period of time.

I have always had real "intent" behind any of my life plans. Yes, some doubt has come in over the years, but it doesn't last long as it's overcome by energy, passion and a will to win. Perhaps it's innate, I'm not entirely sure, but I really don't like to lose at anything. Certainly quitting something goes against the grain for me.

Stubbornness can be a virtue in this regard. The ability to dig my heels in and remain adamant about something. Clearly, it's a two-edged sword and other qualities are required in life. However, I believe a clear and dogged determination to succeed is a great starting point in business.

Chapter 12 – what next for me?

I love being involved with Evolution CBS, but I don't need to run it day in and day out. My Senior Team can do that far better than me. I am now looking for the right person to head up the company so that I can spend more time pursuing a long-held passion.

My original 15-year vision is very much alive. It's been augmented and developed by the woman I married a couple of years ago, Liz, who is a highly creative and intuitive person.

She also came across my forgotten stash 700+ tablets from years ago and together we disposed of them. An immensely liberating experience to feel the release of letting go of the past.

We met in 2012 and two years ago were married on the Greek island of Thassos.

Looking back, one evening, whilst we were in the Aegean, I remember us discussing my passion for teaching English to foreign students. I honestly can't say who came up with an innovative idea, it was probably a creative blend. A cross fertilisation of ideas and thoughts.

Our plan now is to teach English from a Double Decker bus. A mobile language school, bringing much needed additional English to keen and eager Greek children. A big red Double Decker bus going round the island will be a great marketing hook.

Thassos is the size of the Isle of Wight and has a mountain range in the middle of it, with one orbital road going around it. It can take a couple of hours to drive around the island.

Our vision is to take English to the communities on the Island, for children to learn in small classes and all at a discounted price compared to private tuition.

We'll start with teaching English, but it can be expanded to German, French, Swedish, Albanian, Romanian and Bulgarian etc. We already have native speakers, with those languages abilities, wanting to be involved. We'll also employ multi-lingual locals to help with the running the school and to help with any language barriers.

The idea is to start small next year with a summer school, gain some traction and a following on the island, then look to run it throughout the academic year, not just the summer break.

Not me running it, I've learnt how to set something up, then get the right team in place and just oversee it.

I also see this project harmonising with my work with Evolution CBS. I have a vision for flying new clients over to our villa for a day of mentoring and a couple of days sightseeing, then back on a plane to Gatwick. All part of our service to them as clients.

We would have a life split between the UK and Greece, undertaking the work we love, making a difference to people and most of all having fun. This is what I would describe as a true "lifestyle business".

It's something I cover at many of the talks I give around the country; an aspirational lifestyle that enables you to do the things you want to do and when you want to do them. I need to live that message rather than just talk about the theory of it with some PowerPoint slides.

The journey is not over yet, and there have been a number of successes and doubtless there will be more to come. The work will never be completed, we'll just have fresh challenges, new projects, and new people to work with.

Chapter 13 – what next for you?

So where are you in your life journey? Do you have a dream for the future and are you on track? If not, what can you do about it?

When I returned back to the UK from Dubai I had a vision, nothing concrete or certain in terms of detail, but I knew I had to pursue my dreams.

In your life, I have three questions for you;

1. What is your dream?
2. When do you want it to happen?
3. What can you do now to make it happen?

Also, take time to reflect back on the various notes you've written down in this book. How can you take back control in your life so that you can enjoy everything it has to offer? Remember we are dead a long time; enjoy and treasure the life you have been given.

The beautiful island of Thassos

The Thassos "Thinker"

A true lifestyle business

Suggested websites:

The Beermat Entrepreneur
www.beermat.biz

The E-Myth
www.emyth.com

Evolution Complete Business Sales Ltd
www.evolutioncbs.co.uk

Exit Dreams
www.exitdreams.com

Revive your Soul
www.reviveyoursoul.co.uk